Jr. Graphic African-Americ

Nat Turner
and Slave Life on a
Southern Plantation

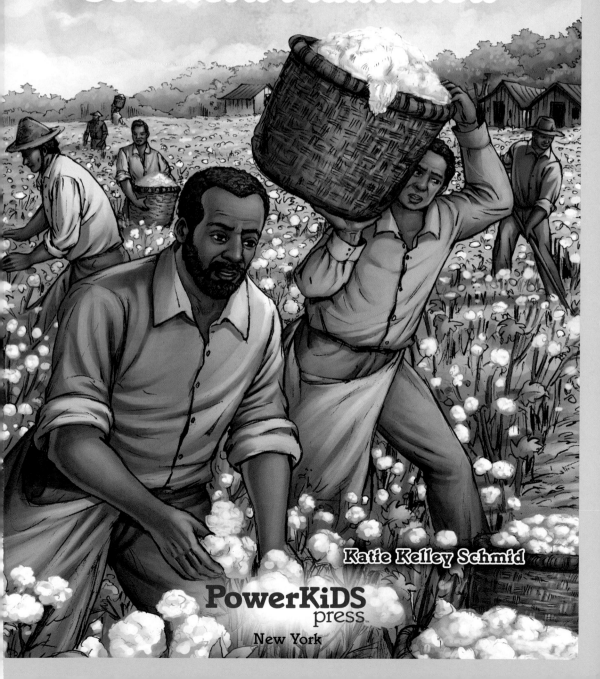

Katie Kelley Schmid

PowerKiDS press

New York

Published in 2014 by The Rosen Publishing Group, Inc.
29 East 21st Street, New York, NY 10010

First Edition

Editor: Joanne Randolph

Book Design: Planman Technologies

Illustrations: Planman Technologies

Library of Congress Cataloging-in-Publication Data

Schmid, Katie Kelley.

Nat Turner and slave life on a southern plantation / by Katie Kelley Schmid. — First edition.

    pages cm. — (Jr. graphic African-American history)

Includes index.

ISBN 978-1-4777-1314-3 (library binding) — ISBN 978-1-4777-1453-9 (pbk.) — ISBN 978-1-4777-1454-6 (6-pack)

1. Turner, Nat, 1800?-1831—Juvenile literature. 2. Southampton Insurrection, 1831—Juvenile literature. 3. Slaves—Virginia—Southampton County— Biography—Juvenile literature. 4. Slave insurrections—Virginia—Southampton County—History—19th century—Juvenile literature. 5. Southampton County (Va.)—History—19th century—Juvenile literature. 6. Turner, Nat, 1800?-1831— Comic books, strips, etc. 7. Southampton Insurrection, 1831—Comic books, strips, etc. 8. Slaves—Virginia—Southampton County—Comic books, strips, etc. 9. Slave insurrections—Virginia—Southampton County—History—19th century—Comic books, strips, etc. 10. Southampton County (Va.)—History— 19th century—Comic books, strips, etc. 11. Graphic novels. I. Title.

F232.S7S45 2014

975.5'5503092—dc23

[B]

2013000193

Manufactured in the United States of America

CPSIA Compliance Information: Batch #S13PK1: For Further Information contact Rosen Publishing, New York, New York at 1-800-237-9932

Contents

Introduction

Nat Turner spent his whole life as an **enslaved** person on **plantations** in Southampton County, Virginia. From a young age, he was religious. Some people thought he would be a **prophet**. Nat believed he had **visions** telling him to rebel against white slave owners. Nat and a band of slaves killed more than 50 white people on August 22 and 23, 1831. The **uprising** became known as Nat Turner's **Rebellion**.

Main Characters

Nat Turner (1800–1831) Enslaved person known for leading a rebellion against white slave owners.

Benjamin Turner (1766–1810) Master of a Southampton, Virginia, plantation and the original owner of Nat.

Samuel Turner (c. 1788–1823) Son of Benjamin Turner and the second master of Nat.

Cherry Turner (unknown) Wife of Nat.

Thomas Moore (unknown–1828) The third owner of Nat. Upon his death, his young son, Putnam, became Nat's master.

Joseph Travis (unknown–1831) Stepfather of Putnam Moore and Nat's last master.

NAT TURNER AND SLAVE LIFE ON A SOUTHERN PLANTATION

NAT TURNER WAS BORN IN 1800 ON BENJAMIN TURNER'S PLANTATION IN SOUTHAMPTON COUNTY, VIRGINIA. HIS MOTHER, NANCY, HAD BEEN CAPTURED IN AFRICA AS A TEENAGER AND SOLD TO BENJAMIN.

NAT SPENT HIS CHILDHOOD SURROUNDED BY OTHER ENSLAVED PEOPLE ON THE PLANTATION. HE WAS TREATED AS A SON BY SOME OF THEM.

AT A YOUNG AGE, NAT TOLD SOME CHILDREN A STORY ABOUT THINGS THAT HAPPENED BEFORE HE WAS BORN.

THAT IS HOW IT HAPPENED. I REMEMBER IT.

NAT, THAT HAPPENED BEFORE YOU WERE BORN. YOU COULD NOT REMEMBER THAT.

WHEN OTHER SLAVES HEARD ABOUT NAT'S STORY, THEY WERE SURPRISED.

THIS CHILD MUST BE A PROPHET. THE LORD HAS SHOWN HIM THINGS THAT HAPPENED BEFORE HE WAS BORN.

YOU WILL SEE. HE IS GOING TO BE A GREAT MAN.

S-T-A-R, STAR. S-K-Y, SKY.

WHO LET HIM TOUCH MY BOOK? SLAVES DON'T KNOW HOW TO READ.

NAT, BEST PUT THAT BOOK DOWN BEFORE YOU GET IN TROUBLE.

ONE DAY, WHEN NAT WAS CRYING, HIS OWNERS GAVE HIM A BOOK. ALTHOUGH NAT DID NOT RECALL LEARNING THE ALPHABET, HE BEGAN SPELLING WORDS.

ON BENJAMIN TURNER'S PLANTATION, MANY SLAVES WORKED THE FIELDS. COTTON AND TOBACCO WERE COMMON CROPS. WORKDAYS FOR SLAVES WERE LONG AND HOT, AND LIFE WAS HARD. SLAVES WERE OFTEN BEATEN IF THEY DISOBEYED OR DID NOT WORK HARD OR FAST ENOUGH.

I LEARNED A NEW SONG TODAY. IT IS ABOUT JESUS AND PLOWING IN THE FIELDS.

RUN ALONG NOW, AND STOP BOTHERING ME. IF I GET CAUGHT LISTENING INSTEAD OF WORKING, I'LL BE WHIPPED.

LISTEN TO THIS SONG ABOUT JESUS.

TEACH US, NAT.

YOUNG SLAVE CHILDREN DID NOT HAVE TO WORK THE FIELDS. THEY COULD PLAY WHILE THEIR PARENTS WORKED. OLDER CHILDREN OFTEN TOOK CARE OF THE YOUNGER CHILDREN.

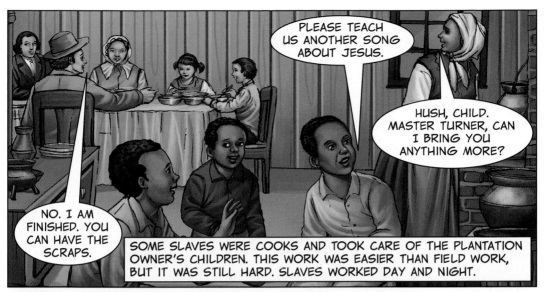

SOME SLAVES WERE COOKS AND TOOK CARE OF THE PLANTATION OWNER'S CHILDREN. THIS WORK WAS EASIER THAN FIELD WORK, BUT IT WAS STILL HARD. SLAVES WORKED DAY AND NIGHT.

OTHER SLAVES WORKED AS HOUSEMAIDS. THEY CLEANED THE HOUSE AND TOOK CARE OF THE PLANTATION.

SOME SLAVES WERE TAUGHT TO WORK AS BLACKSMITHS AND CARPENTERS.

BY THE TIME SLAVE CHILDREN WERE ABOUT 12, THEIR DAYS OF PLAY WERE OVER. THEY WERE EXPECTED TO WORK IN THE FIELDS AND ON THE PLANTATION.

AT LEAST WE CAN SING WHILE WE WORK.

YES, SINGING HELPS THE WORK GO FASTER.

I WONDER HOW THE SEEDS TURN INTO COTTON EACH NOVEMBER. I WANT TO FIND OUT.

NAT, START WORKING. THE OWNER HAS HIS WHIP, AND YOU'LL SOON FEEL IT IF HE SEES YOU JUST LOOKING AT THE COTTON.

EVEN THOUGH HE WAS FORCED TO WORK IN THE FIELDS, NAT STILL WANTED TO LEARN AS MUCH AS HE COULD.

ABOUT THIS TIME, NAT WAS PLACED UNDER AN **OVERSEER**.

I AM GROWN NOW. MASTER TURNER SAID HE WOULD FREE ME.

YOU ARE A SLAVE. I TOLD YOU TO WORK THE FIELDS. YOU'LL DO AS I SAY, AND YOU WILL DO IT NOW.

THE OVERSEER WHIPPED ME, BUT I WAS TOLD I WOULD BE FREED. I DESERVE TO BE FREE.

NAT WAS ANGRY THAT HE HAD NOT BEEN FREED. HE DECIDED TO RUN AWAY.

NAT HID OUT IN THE WOODS FOR 30 DAYS.

THEN NAT FELT HE HAD ANOTHER VISION.

THE SPIRIT TOLD ME TO RETURN TO THE PLANTATION AND DO AS I AM TOLD.

HE RETURNED TO THE PLANTATION. HIS OVERSEER WAS SURPRISED.

THE OTHER SLAVES WERE SHOCKED. THEY THOUGHT NAT HAD ESCAPED TO THE NORTH.

WHY DID YOU COME BACK, NAT? YOU KNOW YOU'LL BE WHIPPED OR THEY'LL CUT OFF YOUR FOOT.

WHAT MATTERS IS THE MASTER IN HEAVEN, NOT THE ONE ON EARTH.

SOMEDAY, CHERRY, WE WILL BE FREED FROM THIS LIFE.

WE WILL DO OUR BEST UNTIL THEN.

SHORTLY AFTER HIS RETURN, NAT MARRIED A SLAVE NAMED CHERRY.

THE FOLLOWING YEAR, SAMUEL TURNER DIED. NAT AND CHERRY WERE SOLD AT A SLAVE AUCTION.

I WILL PURCHASE THE SLAVE CALLED NAT. I DO NOT WANT THE WOMAN.

FORTY DOLLARS FOR THE SLAVE CALLED CHERRY.

NAT: SOLD TO THOMAS MOORE. CHERRY: SOLD TO GILES REESE.

NAT BELIEVED HE HAD SEVERAL VISIONS OVER THE NEXT FEW YEARS. HE CLAIMED TO HAVE EXPERIENCED **MIRACULOUS** EVENTS.

ONE WHITE MAN, ETHELDRED BRANTLEY, WAS GREATLY MOVED BY NAT'S WORDS. HE WANTED TO BE **BAPTIZED**.

NAT CONTINUED TO WORK THE FIELDS AND PREACH TO OTHER SLAVES. WHEN THOMAS MOORE DIED, NAT BECAME THE PROPERTY OF HIS YOUNG SON, PUTNAM. LATER, NAT WAS MOVED TO THE HOME OF JOSEPH TRAVIS, WHO HAD MARRIED THOMAS MOORE'S WIDOW.

NAT BELIEVED A VISION HAD TOLD HIM TO LOOK FOR A SIGN IN THE SKY. WHEN HE SAW IT, HE WAS TO BEGIN A REBELLION AND KILL WHITE SLAVE OWNERS. AN **ECLIPSE** OCCURRED IN FEBRUARY 1831.

NAT MET WITH FOUR OTHER SLAVES: HENRY, HARK, NELSON, AND SAM. HE TOLD THEM ABOUT HIS PLAN FOR KILLING THE SLAVE OWNERS.

I SAW THE SIGN IN THE SKY I HAVE BEEN WAITING FOR. WE MUST PREPARE TO **SLAY** THE ENEMY.

NAT, WE BOTH KNOW WHAT HAPPENS TO SLAVES WHO REBEL, BUT I WILL HELP.

WHEN DO WE BEGIN?

OUR WORK BEGINS ON JULY 4, HARK.

THE MEN TALKED ABOUT WHAT THEY WERE GOING TO DO. HOWEVER, NAT GOT SICK, AND THE GROUP WAS NOT ABLE TO ACT ON THE DATE THEY HAD CHOSEN.

LATER, THE FIVE DECIDED TO MEET ON AUGUST 21. TWO OTHERS JOINED THEM FOR A DINNER BEFORE THEY SET OUT.

I STOLE A PIG FOR THE FEAST.

WHO WANTS SOMETHING TO DRINK?

THE GROUP WAITED UNTIL IT WAS NIGHT. THEN THEY WENT TO THE FIRST HOUSE, **UNARMED**.

FIRST WE WILL GO TO THE TRAVIS HOME.

DO NOT SPARE THE WOMEN AND CHILDREN.

AT EACH HOME, THEY KILLED THE WHITE PEOPLE. THEY ALSO GATHERED UP THE WEAPONS BELONGING TO THE OWNERS.

MASTER TRAVIS HAD FOUR GUNS, SOME **MUSKETS**, AND SOME **GUNPOWDER**. WE WILL GO TO THE FRANCIS HOME NEXT.

THAT NIGHT 50 OR 60 SLAVES JOINED THE REBELLION. MANY WERE ON HORSEBACK.

LET US SPLIT UP. SOME WILL GO TO THE PORTERS'. OTHERS WILL GO TO THE HARRIS HOME. LEAVE THE GILES REESE FAMILY BE.

HURRAH!

NEWS ABOUT THE BAND OF SLAVES ON HORSEBACK BEGAN TRAVELING AROUND THE COMMUNITY. SOME PEOPLE LEFT THEIR HOMES TO TRY TO ESCAPE.

MR. BARROW, DID YOU THINK YOU COULD GET AWAY FROM US?

IN THE MORNING, A GROUP OF WHITE MEN BEGAN PURSUING THE SLAVES.

MY HORSE HAS BEEN HIT.

I HAVE BEEN SHOT.

MANY OF THE SLAVES ABANDONED THE GROUP. OTHERS WERE CAPTURED. THE REBELLION ENDED ON AUGUST 23. MORE THAN 50 PEOPLE HAD BEEN KILLED.

AS SOON AS IT IS DARK, I WILL SNEAK OUT TO GET SOME WATER.

NAT ESCAPED AND HID OUT IN A HOLE FOR SIX WEEKS. ON OCTOBER 30, A DOG DISCOVERED HIS HIDING PLACE. NAT WAS CAPTURED AT GUNPOINT AND TAKEN TO JAIL.

DO YOU KNOW OF ANY **CONCERTED** PLAN OF THE SLAVES TO KILL THEIR MASTERS?

I DO NOT.

WHILE IN JAIL, NAT SPENT FOUR DAYS GIVING HIS **CONFESSION** TO THOMAS GRAY. THE CONFESSION WOULD BE PUBLISHED A MONTH LATER.

THE NEXT DAY, NAT WAS TRIED.

NAT TURNER! STAND UP. HAVE YOU ANY THING TO SAY WHY SENTENCE OF DEATH SHOULD NOT BE PRONOUNCED AGAINST YOU?

I HAVE MADE A FULL CONFESSION TO MR. GRAY, AND I HAVE NOTHING MORE TO SAY.

THE JUDGMENT OF THE COURT IS ON FRIDAY NEXT YOU BE HUNG! MAY THE LORD HAVE MERCY UPON YOUR SOUL.

ON NOVEMBER 11, NAT WAS HANGED.

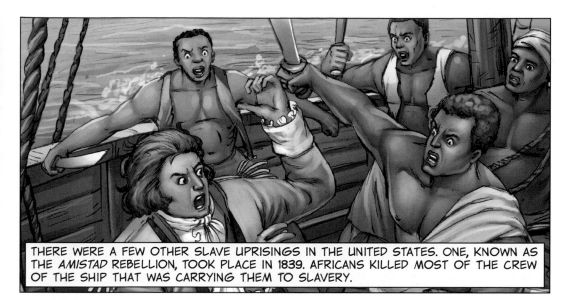

THERE WERE A FEW OTHER SLAVE UPRISINGS IN THE UNITED STATES. ONE, KNOWN AS THE *AMISTAD* REBELLION, TOOK PLACE IN 1839. AFRICANS KILLED MOST OF THE CREW OF THE SHIP THAT WAS CARRYING THEM TO SLAVERY.

MANY SLAVES ATTEMPTED TO ESCAPE SECRETLY VIA THE UNDERGROUND RAILROAD RATHER THAN BY REBELLING.

GET IN THIS WAGON. IT WILL TAKE YOU TO THE NEXT STATION.

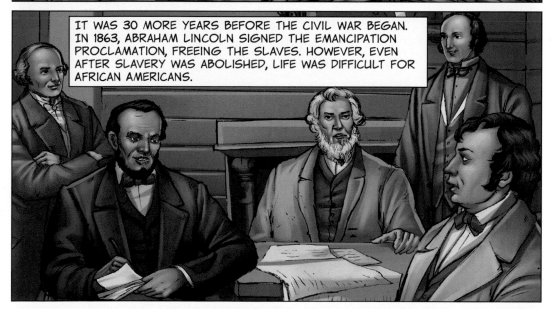

IT WAS 30 MORE YEARS BEFORE THE CIVIL WAR BEGAN. IN 1863, ABRAHAM LINCOLN SIGNED THE EMANCIPATION PROCLAMATION, FREEING THE SLAVES. HOWEVER, EVEN AFTER SLAVERY WAS ABOLISHED, LIFE WAS DIFFICULT FOR AFRICAN AMERICANS.

Timeline

1800	Nat Turner is born in Southampton County, Virginia. He is the property of Benjamin Turner.
1809	Nat's ownership is transferred to Benjamin's son, Samuel.
1810	Benjamin Turner dies.
1817	Nat begins having visions.
1821	Nat runs away after a whipping. He returns 30 days later.
1822	Nat marries Cherry.
1823	Samuel Turner dies. Nat and Cherry are sold to different owners.
1828	Nat's owner, Thomas Moore, dies. Nat becomes the property of 6-year-old Putnam Moore.
February 12, 1831	There is an eclipse of the sun, which Nat believes is a sign to lead a rebellion.
August 22, 1831	Nat leads a group of slaves against their white owners.
August 23, 1831	The rebellion ends. Some slaves are captured. Nat goes into hiding.
October 30, 1831	Nat's hiding place is found. He is captured.
November 1–4, 1831	Nat and Thomas Gray compile Nat's confessions.
November 5, 1831	At his trial, Nat is found guilty.
November 11, 1831	Nat is hanged.
December 1831	"The Confessions of Nat Turner, The Leader of the Late Insurrections in Southampton, Va." is published.
1861	The Civil War begins.
1865	The Civil War ends. Slavery is abolished.

Glossary

baptized (BAP-tyzd) Sprinkled with or immersed in water to show acceptance into the Christian faith.

concerted (kon-SER-tid) Planned or arranged together.

confession (kun-FEH-shun) Telling the truth about something.

eclipse (ih-KLIPS) A darkening of the sun or the moon that occurs when the light of the sun is blocked by the moon or when the light of the moon is blocked by Earth's shadow.

enslaved (en-SLAYVD) Made someone be a slave.

gunpowder (GUN-pow-dur) A black powder that explodes in a gun and moves the bullet.

miraculous (mer-AK-yoo-lus) Suggesting a miracle, a wonderful or an unusual event said to have been done by God.

muskets (MUS-kits) Long-barreled firearms used by soldiers before the invention of the rifle.

overseer (OH-ver-see-ur) A person who watches over workers.

plantations (plan-TAY-shunz) Large farms where crops are grown.

prophet (PRAH-fet) Someone who says he or she brings messages from God.

rebellion (rih-BEL-yun) A fight against one's government.

revelation (rev-uh-LAY-shun) An act of revealing or making known divine truth.

slay (SLAY) Kill.

unarmed (un-ARMD) Not using or involving a weapon.

uprising (UP-ry-zing) Act of rising up, opposing authority.

visions (VIH-zhenz) Things seen in the mind (as during a dream).

Index

Websites

Due to the changing nature of Internet links, PowerKids Press has developed an online list of websites related to the subject of this book. This site is updated regularly. Please use this link to access the list:

www.powerkidslinks.com/jgaah/life/